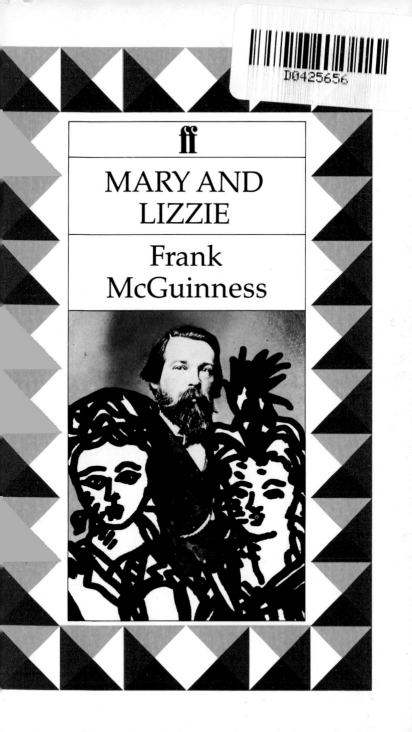

ff

MARY AND LIZZIE

Frank McGuinness

MARY AND LIZZIE

Born in Buncrana, Co. Donegal, Frank McGuinness now lives in Dublin and lectures in English at St Patrick's College, Maynooth. He has also worked at the University of Ulster, Coleraine and at University College, Dublin.

For the Abbey Theatre he has written *The Factory Girls*, *Baglady/Ladybag* and in 1985 the celebrated *Observe the Sons of Ulster Marching Towards the Somme* which won many awards, including the London Standard Most Promising Playwright Award, an Arts Council bursary, the Rooney Prize for Irish Literature, the 1985 Harvey's Best Play Award and the Cheltenham Literary Prize.

His play *Innocence* (on the life of Caravaggio) premièred at the Gate Theatre in October 1986. His new version of Lorca's *Yerma* was produced at the Abbey Theatre in May 1987 and a new version of Ibsen's *Rosmersholm*, commissioned by the National Theatre of Great Britain, opened in the same week. He has written a version of *Peer Gynt* for the Gate Theatre.

Carthaginians received its première during the 1988 Dublin Theatre Festival, and was also produced at Hampstead Theatre.

MARY
AND
LIZZIE

FRANK McGUINNESS

faber and faber
LONDON · BOSTON

First published in 1989
by Faber and Faber Limited
3 Queen Square, London WCIN 3AU

Photoset by Parker Typesetting Service Leicester
Printed in Great Britain by
Richard Clay Ltd Bungay Suffolk

ISBN 0–571–14268–0

For Peter Holmes

CHARACTERS

MARY BURNS
LIZZIE BURNS, her sister
THE WOMEN IN THE TREES
A PREGNANT GIRL
AN OLD WOMAN, Mother Ireland
A PRIEST
MOTHER, to Mary and Lizzie
THE WOMEN OF THE FAMINE
A PIG
QUEEN VICTORIA
KARL MARX
FREDERICK ENGELS
FATHER, to Mary and Lizzie
JENNY MARX
A BOY
THE WOMEN OF THE CAMPS

Mary and Lizzie was first performed by the Royal Shakespeare Company in the Pit at the Barbican, London on 27 September 1989. The cast was as follows:

MARY BURNS	Maureen Beattie
LIZZIE BURNS	Lesley Sharp
A PREGNANT GIRL	Cate Hamer
AN OLD WOMAN	Pip Hinton
A PRIEST	Nicholas Woodeson
MOTHER	Darlene Johnson
A PIG	Robert Demenger
QUEEN VICTORIA	Nicholas Woodeson
KARL MARX	Simon Dormandy
FREDERICK ENGELS	Simon Russell Beale
FATHER	Robert Demenger
JENNY MARX	Katy Behean
A BOY	Timothy Stark
CHORUS	Jane Cox, Caroline Harding, Maggie Carr, Kate Byers, Candida Gubbins, Louise Kerr

Director	Sarah Pia Anderson
Designer	Ultz
Lighting	Geraint Pughe
Music	Shaun Davy
Stage Management	Jan Bevis Hughes, Richard Reddrop, Sarah Cox

The author acknowledges the assistance of all who participated in the workshop on *Mary and Lizzie*, organized by the RSC, at Stratford-upon-Avon, in July 1988.

LIZZIE: They say long ago in this country there was a city of
women who lived in the trees. They'd followed soldiers who
they believed loved them. At the camp they were received
like lepers and were banished into the forest. Fleas ate them,
and they drew blood, scratching the world from themselves,
weeping up the trees like withered leaves in rain.

(*A community of women. They live in the trees. They sing.*)

WOMEN: Sén trua nach mise, nach mise,
Sén trua nach mise Bean Phaidín.
Sén trua nach mise, nach mise,
Sén trua nach mise Bean Phaidín.

LIZZIE: The next thing I knew this man was beside me.

WOMEN: How did you know?

LIZZIE: It wasn't his face. The next thing I knew my fingers were
moving.

WOMEN: How did they move?

LIZZIE: They knew their way home.

WOMEN: Sén trua, nach mise, nach mise,
Sén trua nach mise Bean Phaidín.

LIZZIE: The next thing I knew my fingers were bleeding.

WOMEN: How did they bleed?

LIZZIE: Red roaring red. The next thing I knew his heart was
beating. How did I know? It wasn't my own. The next thing
I knew his fist was inside me.

WOMEN: How did you know?

LIZZIE: It cut like a knife. The next thing I knew his voice was
like honey.

WOMEN: How did you know?

LIZZIE: Sweet in my mouth.

(LIZZIE *starts to climb the trees. The* WOMEN *sing.*)

WOMEN: Sén trua nach mise, nach mise,
Sén trua nach mise Bean Phaidín.

LIZZIE: The next thing I knew the girl, she was rising. Up to the

I

stars and into the moon. The man he came following, following, following, with his fist raised to the sun.

(LIZZIE *moves from tree to tree.*)

WOMEN: Run, girl, run, run.

(MARY *enters on the earth. She sings low.*)

MARY: Sén trua nach mise, nach mise,
    Sén trua nach mise Bean Phaidín.

(*Silence.*)

LIZZIE: Mary?

MARY: Lizzie.

LIZZIE: How are you here?

MARY: I followed you.

LIZZIE: Why?

MARY: We've work to do away from here.

LIZZIE: Such as what?

MARY: Wander the earth.

LIZZIE: Do it yourself.

MARY: Where you are, I am.

LIZZIE: How did you find me?

MARY: I heard your heart beating.

LIZZIE: How did you hear?

MARY: It was near breaking. Will I show you your heart?

(*A* PREGNANT GIRL *enters. She carries a bayonet.*)

PREGNANT GIRL: My name is gone, my good name.

(*The* WOMEN *mock the girl.*)

FIRST WOMAN: My name's gone.

SECOND WOMAN: Gone, gone.

THIRD WOMAN: She's wearing clothes.

FOURTH WOMAN: Woman's clothes.

FIFTH WOMAN: She's a woman.

SIXTH WOMAN: My name's gone.

FIRST WOMAN: Strap her down.

SECOND WOMAN: Strip her naked.

THIRD WOMAN: Strap her.

FOURTH WOMAN: Naked, strap her naked.

FIFTH WOMAN: Strip her.

PREGNANT GIRL: They won't let me in, they won't let me in.

MARY: In where?

2

PREGNANT GIRL: In at the camp, the army camp. My man said to follow his regiment. I'd find him waiting at the Curragh camp. But they won't let me in. They gave me this weapon. (*Raises the bayonet.*) They sent me here, bag and baggage, they won't let me in.

MARY: How far are you gone?

(*The women whistle.*)

WOMEN: How far are you gone? How far are you gone?

LIZZIE: Are you lonely down there, Mary?

FIRST WOMAN: Can you climb a tree?

SECOND WOMAN: Leave her behind you.

THIRD WOMAN: The one carrying death.

FOURTH WOMAN: When it dies, she'll rise among us.

FIFTH WOMAN: Do you see us in heaven?

SIXTH WOMAN: Will you stand with the saints?

FIRST WOMAN: The saints on the cross.

MARY: Lizzie.

SECOND WOMAN: Who is she?

LIZZIE: My sister.

THIRD WOMAN: No such thing here.

FOURTH WOMAN: Only wind, rain and water.

FIFTH WOMAN: Smell of sight and smell of sound.

SIXTH WOMAN: Waiting here for a good hiding.

FIRST WOMAN: But at least it's the touch of a man. Get the one carrying a bastard.

(*The* WOMEN *tumble to the earth. They surround the* PREGNANT GIRL. *They threaten her with the bayonet. All the time they howl the word 'run'. The bayonet suddenly falls. The* PREGNANT GIRL *is still. The* WOMEN *separate about her in silence. The* FIRST WOMAN *starts to weep. She raises both her hands.*)

Where are my hands?

SECOND WOMAN: You cut them off to send to your soldier.

THIRD WOMAN: So he could find his touch upon you.

(*The* FIRST WOMAN *shows her tongue.*)

FIRST WOMAN: Where is my tongue?

FOURTH WOMAN: You bit to its root and spat it from you.

FIFTH WOMAN: The last words of love would be to your man.

3

FIRST WOMAN: Where are the legs that walked after him?

SIXTH WOMAN: You took an axe and chopped them off you.

FIRST WOMAN: Here I would stay until he returned.

PREGNANT GIRL: Where is he?

FIRST WOMAN: Where yours is.

PREGNANT GIRL: How long have you waited?

FIRST WOMAN: How old is the earth? It must be ancient. Old as the hills. He never returned. Tell her our story. All the one story. Tell her.

LIZZIE: Who?

FIRST WOMAN: You, Lizzie Burns. Who still has a name. You'll lose it, like we lost ours, so speak, before it's lost.
  (LIZZIE *sings*.)

LIZZIE: I courted a soldier who loved another,
   Neither father nor mother, sister nor brother,
   For love it is lonely, looks for no shelter,
   Content in itself, though inclined to wander.

   The soldier went walking through lands barren
   And followed the road of the sparrow and wren.
   In trees I searched for him, through leaves hidden,
   For my love he chased the hare from its den.

   My love when he left me promised jewels,
   Bracelets and bangles and soft silver bells,
   But love it is lonely, inclined to be cruel,
   The gem that it gives is the burning swell.

   And soldiers go walking through lands barren
   And follow the road of the sparrow and wren.
   In trees we search for them, through leaves hidden,
   For my love he chased the hare from its den.
  (*Silence*.)

PREGNANT GIRL: Have you ever killed anything?

FIRST WOMAN: A bird. A young one. I laid the egg. I smashed it against the wall. Wrung its neck with a cord. Left it in the trees, lamenting. Curse that carcass from you.
  (MARY BURNS *lifts the bayonet*.)

4

MARY: Or carry it.
  (*She turns it towards herself.*)
  Carry your burden until it's time to cut it from you, let it fly.
  (*She plunges it into her body. She removes it, unbloodied.*)
  If it's alive, it's only yourself.
  (*She is unmarked.*)
FIRST WOMAN: I saw you kill –
MARY: Nothing.
FIRST WOMAN: You killed –
MARY: I killed nothing. You killed nothing.
FIRST WOMAN: A child. It was mine, red. A man took me.
MARY: You gave your body.
FIRST WOMAN: My body?
MARY: Your body. You gave your body.
FIRST WOMAN: No such thing. Nothing. Get you and your sister
  and your name out of where none of you belong. You are a
  dead woman.
MARY: So are you.
  (MARY *holds out her hands to* LIZZIE. LIZZIE *shakes her head.*
  MARY *withdraws her hands.* LIZZIE *walks to her. The*
  PREGNANT GIRL *sits crouched, nursing the bayonet.* MARY *and*
  LIZZIE *kiss. The* WOMEN *in the trees vanish.*)
LIZZIE: Kiss and tell.

2 THE EARTH OPENS

MARY *and* LIZZIE *walk back and forth.*

LIZZIE: They say long ago in this world there were two women,
Mary and Lizzie Burns. Why were they in this world? To
wander it. Wander through time, through place, for that was
their way, their story. This is the telling of Mary and Lizzie,
and the ways they walked through lives together.
(*An* OLD WOMAN *enters, singing.*)
OLD WOMAN: Fill, fill a ṙun Ó,
Fill, a ṙun Ó, is na imigh uaim,
Fill ort a chuid de'n saol mhór
No chár fhéiceann tú nglóir mur bfilleodh tú.

Turn, return, my grace, my stór,
Turn, my own, do not leave me,
Turn, return, to heaven's door,
See me, my son, do not grieve me.

You've betrayed Peter, you've betrayed Paul,
Betrayed priest and pope for gold,
The keys of the kingdom you've let fall,
Turn to me, son, before the grave cold.

Turn, return, my grace, my stór,
Turn, my own, do not leave me,
Turn, return, to heaven's door,
See me, my son, do not grieve me.
(*The* OLD WOMAN *stops singing.*)
OLD WOMAN: This land's mine. What's mine is yours.
MARY: We don't want land.
OLD WOMAN: I'm worth my weight in gold and silver.
LIZZIE: We want neither.
OLD WOMAN: Then what can I give you? Do you like men?
MARY: Yes.

6

OLD WOMAN: Do you have faith in men?

LIZZIE: Yes.

OLD WOMAN: I had a son who was beautiful.

MARY: Kind?

LIZZIE: Good?

OLD WOMAN: Are you hungry?

LIZZIE: Yes.

OLD WOMAN: Shall I feed you?

LIZZIE: What with?

OLD WOMAN: A song for your throat.

LIZZIE: The hunger's here.

(LIZZIE *touches her belly*.)

OLD WOMAN: Have you known a man?

(*Silence*.)

What's a man to you?

LIZZIE: Strong.

MARY: A song.

OLD WOMAN: I choose you for my son.

MARY: Choose both or neither.

OLD WOMAN: Better be both, for my son's lost. Lost the keys of the kingdom. He's betrayed Peter and Paul. Betrayed priest and pope. Commit the sin of lust with my beautiful son. Follow me to him.

MARY: Where is he?

(*The* OLD WOMAN *produces a golden key*.)

OLD WOMAN: Locked in the house this key opens. He converted from Catholic to Protestant. I close my eyes when I see him now. Sin with my son. Then he'll seek his penance. Before a holy priest. Heaven's door he's slammed shut in his face and the gates of Hell stand open before him. Follow me.

MARY: Not until I know which direction. Where's the door this key opens?

(*On the earth the* OLD WOMAN *makes the sign of the cross with the key. She places the key in the centre of the imaginary cross. The earth opens*.)

LIZZIE: It's a grave.

(*The* OLD WOMAN *shakes her head*.)

She's the devil.

(The OLD WOMAN *laughs*.)
Don't go with her.

OLD WOMAN: She'll come.

LIZZIE: No.

OLD WOMAN: She'll love my beautiful son.
   (*The* OLD WOMAN *climbs into the earth*.)

MARY: Maybe it's home, Lizzie.

LIZZIE: In a grave?

MARY: It's only the earth.

LIZZIE: I'm afraid of the grave. It's where I was born. Our
   mother died when she gave me birth. Mary, what did she
   look like?

MARY: Come and see.
   (MARY *and* LIZZIE *enter the earth*.)

PRIEST: Praise be to Christ who is King of the waters, mighty and wonderful in earth and water. Lead me, Aquinas, who doth walk in love and knowledge. Hear me, great Luther, in faith's defence. Shelter me, Calvin, in fate and fortitude. A mighty tower let me construct, an alphabet of God, ye prophets of Revelations. Let me recite for my people a service of splendour that they shall eat the fruits of love, of good and evil. From my hand and my mouth shall speak such truths that they who witness shall feel their breath turn to fire. And from this divine service I shall exclude my mother.

Turn, turn, ye Catholic damned, fear, fear for the error of your ways, fear as I feared for my many errors. I gave this body to the whore of Babylon, robed in the regalia of Catholic priests. I wear these raiments as penance and punishment. I saw the light that is Satan's throne. Children of Ireland, have you seen Satan? Children of Ireland, have you seen my mother? Do not listen to her lies and scandals. I am no Catholic, no Protestant. I worship both faiths with new eyes.

Shall I spell out the faith of the future? Christ is amongst us with a new commandment. Hate one another as I have hated you. Jesus it was who tempted Satan, promised him the throne of Rome. Satan agreed on one condition. Amend the commandments of the Lord. In this island I preach new religion. Where there is God, take his name in vain. Remember thou keep the Sabbath savage. Kill the honour of father and mother. Steal neighbour's wife and neighbour's goods. Convert, convert and covet, covet.

(*Enter* OLD WOMAN.)

Wash ye in waters of revelation, dance in the beauty of virgin's blood.

OLD WOMAN: Jesus, Mary and St Joseph.

PRIEST: Fear not the dawn of holy salvation, embrace the night of your new soul.

9

OLD WOMAN: Have you been reading that unfortunate Bible?

PRIEST: Christ is amongst us, the beast and the beauty, come to his house and covet conversion.

OLD WOMAN: Curse be the day I came across this.

PRIEST: You wouldn't have if you hadn't been spying.

OLD WOMAN: I was right to watch you like a hawk.

PRIEST: A singularly appropriate bird of prey, mother. Pray? No sense of humour, Catholics.

OLD WOMAN: Have I lived to see one of mine turn?

PRIEST: Yes, you have, mother dear. Turn from blind faith to a wise one. I have been Catholic, I have been Protestant, now I am both and wish you were too.

OLD WOMAN: Never.

PRIEST: Please yourself. But I sent you on business. Did you fetch me a cobweb?

(MARY *and* LIZZIE *enter*.)

OLD WOMAN: Here are two spiders, son.

PRIEST: Mother, they are women.

OLD WOMAN: Fine women.

PRIEST: I've noticed. You've wasted your time coming here. I'm spoken for. It's time Mother Ireland accepted that. The amount of girls she's encouraged to climb through the earth – astonishing really. I take it she has informed you of her mystical plan? She finds a nice girl, I fuck her, fall into despair over broken vows of chastity, return to the Catholics, abandon Protestantism, do my penance and forget my allegiance to the religion I've founded? Then all's well, yes? No go, Mother dear. Not interested. Would you excuse me, I've to say Mass. Black Mass, that is.

OLD WOMAN: My son died and this was put in his place.

PRIEST: She's mad.

OLD WOMAN: Love him.

MARY: Why?

PRIEST: Yes, why, Mother?

OLD WOMAN: He needs a woman.

MARY: He needs a wife.

PRIEST: I like her. She has brains. They'll be delicious fried in a little butter. We eat them in our religious sacrifices, the handmaidens who climb down here. Good hunting, Mother. (*Points at* LIZZIE.) A leg will do nicely, and a little slice of lung.

LIZZIE: I won't be eaten.

PRIEST: Don't be difficult. Tears distress me. I know they're necessary. We collect them, you know. I pour them into a chalice and offer them up as a gift to my God from the poor of the Irish people, who will always be with us. Silly saying really, not one of your best, Jesus, it only encourages the buggers.

LIZZIE: If I were to convert –

PRIEST: To my strange religion, which is the destiny of Ireland? A killing combination of two defunct faiths that can only survive by feeding off each other? Forgive me, I'm getting carried away by my vision of the future. You were saying?

LIZZIE: If I were to convert, would you still kill me?

PRIEST: Yes, lucky you. Straight ascent to Heaven. No questions asked. So do convert, my dear – what is your name, child?

LIZZIE: Lizzie Burns.

PRIEST: Charming.

LIZZIE: When I was twelve I saw the Devil.

PRIEST: What was he like?

LIZZIE: It was a she.

PRIEST: What was she like?

(LIZZIE *points to* MARY.)

LIZZIE: Her.

MARY: Say the Black Mass.

PRIEST: Why?

MARY: In my honour.

PRIEST: I can't. I'm no longer a priest.

OLD WOMAN: Once a priest, always a priest, my beautiful son.

MARY: Yes, he is beautiful. Shall we marry him?

LIZZIE: Shall we eat him?

PRIEST: Mother, do something.

MARY: His lungs and kidneys.

PRIEST: They belong to God. I belong to God.

LIZZIE: His legs and arms.

PRIEST: God's terribly possessive.

II

MARY: His feet.

LIZZIE: His hair.

MARY: His heart.

LIZZIE: His eyes.

MARY: His soul.

LIZZIE: Yes, his soul.

MARY: He's signed away his soul.

LIZZIE: Let's eat his soul.

PRIEST: You'll have to find it first.

MARY: It's in my pocket.

LIZZIE: It's up my skirt.

MARY: Between the two of us.

PRIEST: Mother.

OLD WOMAN: Good girls, keep going.

MARY: Bite us and draw blood.

LIZZIE: We're poor lost Catholics.

MARY: We want to convert.

LIZZIE: Convert you, body and soul.

PRIEST: O Jesus.

MARY: Your sweet Protestant soul.

LIZZIE: Your strong Catholic body.

PRIEST: Why did you bring them here?

LIZZIE: We came of our own accord, Mary and Lizzie.

PRIEST: Would you like a Bible?

MARY: We can't read.

LIZZIE: We don't want to.

MARY: We want to get married.

PRIEST: Then do, do.

OLD WOMAN: They want to marry you, pet.

PRIEST: I'm married to myself.

OLD WOMAN: And you never said?

PRIEST: It came as quite a shock to me.

OLD WOMAN: When did this happen?

PRIEST: The day I converted. I was Catholic and Protestant. I'm a mixed marriage, Mother.

OLD WOMAN: And you see where it's led you.

PRIEST: Yes.

OLD WOMAN: You broke my heart. Why?

PRIEST: It's a mystery, Mother.

OLD WOMAN: No more mysteries. No more marriages.

MARY: Marry me.

PRIEST: Who to?

MARY: Myself.

LIZZIE: Marry me.

PRIEST: Who to?

LIZZIE: My mother.

PRIEST: I don't have the words to either ceremony.

MARY: Make them up as you go along.

PRIEST: Do you, Mary Burns, take this woman, Mary Burns, to be your lawful wedded wife?

MARY: I do.

PRIEST: To have and to hold, in sickness and in health, till death do you part?

MARY: I do.

PRIEST: I now pronounce you woman and wife. And do you, Lizzie Burns, take your mother as your lawful wedded wife? (*Silence.*)
Well?

LIZZIE: I want to see her.

PRIEST: Beyond my power.
(*The* PRIEST *and the* OLD WOMAN *fade.*)

LIZZIE: She's dead. She's in the grave. And we're in the earth. We can meet here. Show me her. Mother.

MARY: She'll come.

LIZZIE: Why?

MARY: You've called her.

LIZZIE: What did she look like?

MARY: Look.

There is baroque music. The MOTHER *is attended by six* WOMEN *in elaborate, jewelled costume. The* WOMEN *carry six covered gold platters. At the click of the mother's fingers, the music ceases. The mother stares at* MARY *and* LIZZIE.

MOTHER: Yous pick your time to call, what do yous want? I'm watching over you morning, noon and night but of course that's not enough. Oh no, the old horse here can't get a minute's peace. What are you looking at with them sheep's eyes?

LIZZIE: Is it you?

MOTHER: As far as I know. Look at the cut of them, shame a body. Do something with your hair. Like comb it. Two bales of hay. If I had lived to rear you, you wouldn't be out like that. Nothing I can do now. You're old enough and ugly enough to know better.

LIZZIE: We're not ugly.

MOTHER: Listen to that. Better fit for you to offer your dead mother a chair. Never mind, I'll stay on my feet.

LIZZIE: I'll find you a chair.

MOTHER: I don't want a chair.

LIZZIE: Do you want a chair?

MOTHER: I said I didn't.

LIZZIE: She wants a chair.

MOTHER: You couldn't like that one if you'd just given birth to her.

LIZZIE: You gave birth to me.

MOTHER: I know, I died. I was tired. And I couldn't watch you die. You might have. Two others did.

LIZZIE: Mary lived.

MOTHER: Mary was Mary.

LIZZIE: Who was I?

MOTHER: The last born. It does funny things to a woman, birth. You choose your time to live and die. When you arrived, I chose to go. I let you live. I gave you my life. Don't bother thanking me. I wanted out of this world. Heaven's great, girls, best of everything. Are yous married yet?

MARY: No.

MOTHER: Don't. And don't have children. They kill you. Look at these, God love them. (*Points to the* WOMEN) Every one, died at childbirth.

LIZZIE: How?

MOTHER: They could see the future. When I had you last, I saw my future – one daughter after another until the end of my time. I'd had enough, so I closed my two eyes. Same with them. But they saw more than their own death coming. It's bad news for this country. I want yous out of it. Go to England now.

LIZZIE: We can't speak English.

MOTHER: What in God's name do you think you're talking in?

LIZZIE: Gaelic.

MOTHER: Dead as a duck. Forget it. I've arranged for you to be given the gift of tongues. I want no thanks. Think of it as a Christening present. You were beautiful when you were born. So was Mary. So were the dead ones. Ah well, no point lamenting.

LIZZIE: I love you.

MOTHER: Are you looking for something?

LIZZIE: Nothing.

MOTHER: Just as well. That's what's in store for you here. If you stay.

LIZZIE: I want to stay.

MOTHER: Well, if you won't listen to me, maybe you'll listen to strangers, then. Tell them what's coming to poor old Ireland.

FIRST WOMAN: Famine.

SECOND WOMAN: Death.

THIRD WOMAN: Disease.

FOURTH WOMAN: Exile.

FIFTH WOMAN: Hunger.

SIXTH WOMAN: Fever.

MOTHER: The girls are a bit on the gloomy side, but they know what they're talking about. Show them. Listen, have you

15

eaten? Here's the feast of famine. Music for the feast.
(*A slow lament begins. The* FIRST WOMAN *lifts the platter's lid
to show a stone. The* SECOND WOMAN *shows a book. The*
THIRD WOMAN *shows rags. The* FOURTH WOMAN *shows a
spoon. The* FIFTH WOMAN *shows a straw. The* SIXTH WOMAN
shows a bone. The PREGNANT GIRL *enters, carrying a cauldron
and a bayonet. The* WOMEN *sing separately.*)

FIRST WOMAN: If this stone could speak, it would say,
    Throw me in the pot, throw me in the pot.
SECOND WOMAN: If this book were read, it would write,
    Throw me in the pot, throw me in the pot.
THIRD WOMAN: Were I these rags, I would ask,
    Throw me in the pot, throw me in the pot.
FOURTH WOMAN: This spoon wants a mouth to shout,
    Throw me in the pot, throw me in the pot.
FIFTH WOMAN: I lay on straw and heard it sigh,
    Throw me in the pot, throw me in the pot.
SIXTH WOMAN: My child shrank from skin to bone,
    Throw me in the pot, throw me in the pot.
    (*During the song, the* PREGNANT GIRL *has collected the objects
    into her cauldron. She stirs the ingredients with the bayonet. The*
    WOMEN *sing.*)
WOMEN: When it's dead, boil its head,
    Make it into soup and bread.
    When it's dead, boil its head,
    Make it into soup and bread.
FIRST WOMAN: Soup of stone and bread of straw,
    Eat the rat, the field, the haw.
SECOND WOMAN: Bread of bone and bread of rags,
    Eat the dead of starving hags.
THIRD WOMAN: Head of stone and empty spoon,
    Eat the stars and belly's wound.
    (*The* WOMEN *sing.*)
WOMEN: Do this all of you in memory
    Of the race hunger freed.
    Do this all of you in memory
    Of the race that ate its seed.
    Do this all of you in memory

Of the race that died in need.

FOURTH WOMAN: Here the roadside, here the cabin,
Here the dying, dying millions.

FIFTH WOMAN: Here the fever, here the din
Of the dying, dying millions.

SIXTH WOMAN: Here the hands stretched in pain
From the dying, dying millions.

(*From the cauldron the* PREGNANT GIRL *takes out potatoes. She cuts them with the bayonet.*)

MOTHER: It will fail, the potato crop, girls. There'll be famine. It will spread through the land. There will be neither warning nor consolation. Blight will fall from sky to soil. A million dead. A million gone to foreign lands. Get you now to your father. England is no promised land. But they look after their own. You'll have the bite in your stomach. Leave here before the earth devours its young and old.

(*The* MOTHER *sings. The* PREGNANT GIRL *stirs the cauldron. As the* MOTHER *sings, the* PREGNANT GIRL *serves her cauldron to the* WOMEN, *who drink emptiness from it.*)

Soup of stone and bread of straw,
Eat the rat, the field, the haw.
Bread of bone and head of rags,
Eat the dead of starving hags.
Head of stone and empty spoon,
Eat the stars and belly's wound.
Remember feast, remember famine,
Famine feast and feast of famine.
Times of want, times of plenty,
The gentleman who pays the rent,
The gentleman who pays the rent.

(*The music turns into a reel. A* PIG *appears, dressed as a Victorian gentleman. The* PIG *dances with the* MOTHER. *The* WOMEN *look on, beating time with the lid of the platters.*)

PIG: Tell them who I am, good woman.

MOTHER: A pig.

PIG: A special pig.

MOTHER: A dancing pig.

PIG: A speaking pig.

17

MOTHER: A gentleman pig.

PIG: Ladies, I have not made my introductions. Forgive me. (*Bows*) In Ireland I am called the gentleman who pays the rent. And so I am well treated. I'm not for eating, I'm for exporting. Have you heard of landlords? Well, I line their pockets. But pigs are of passing interest to you humans. Self, self, self, that's all you think about. I'll never understand you. We're born to die, but you keep asking, why am I here, why am I here? By the way, why am I here?

MOTHER: It's the feast of famine.

PIG: Ah yes, famine. Terrible. Strange thing is, we animals saw it coming, but would you believe our signs? I myself composed a little verse or two on the whole tragic topic, but unfortunately I was shipped off to the Saxon shores before publication were possible. I threw it into a passing cargo ship, you know, the ones with rotten flour so generously bestowed for famine relief, but I'm sure no one found it and the poem is lost for ever.

MOTHER: Have you forgotten it?

PIG: I remember every word.

MOTHER: Tell us.

(*The* PIG *clears his throat, and recites.*)

PIG:
   In the most distressing country that ever has been seen,
   Lived a lovely little family, we shall call the family Green,
   They had a little cabin and a little bit of land,
   And they worked and worked it until they could barely
      stand.
   They lived on spuds and buttermilk and a little bit of fish,
   And the rest of what they grew made the landlord's dainty
      dish.
   They had children who had children who had children
      with child,
   And the children of these children grew exceedingly wild.
   And to curb this population the Good Lord sent a plague,
   They grew thinner and thinner in arm and in leg.

   In the most distressing country that ever has been seen
   Died a lovely little family, they all had turned quite green,

For a great big butcher came along holding up a knife,
And they screamed for mercy, they screamed for dear life.
We'll call the butcher empire and the knife we'll call its
    greed,
And it cut the throat of Ireland, leaving it to bleed.
But what care for the Irish, aren't they dirty pigs?
Leave them in their squalor to dance their Irish jigs.
Wash your hands and wash your hands and wash hands
    again
Of the blood and the fever and leave no sign of stain.

Good friends and true friends, listen to my tale,
Here for you's a moral that never fails,
God protects the rich and the rich protect themselves,
The poor can go hang and the Irish go to Hell.

(*The* PIG *bows. The* PREGNANT GIRL *approaches him. She slits his throat with the bayonet. The* PIG *squeals in horror and runs off. The* PREGNANT GIRL *approaches* MARY *and* LIZZIE.)

MARY: What are you carrying in your belly?

PREGNANT GIRL: A stone to build my house.

(*She hands* MARY *the stone.*)

LIZZIE: What's in the house?

PREGNANT GIRL: A book to say I live there.

(*She hands* LIZZIE *the book.*)

MARY: How will you live?

PREGNANT GIRL: In rags and in want.

(*She hands* MARY *the rags.*)

LIZZIE: What will you want?

PREGNANT GIRL: A spoon to stir my sorrow.

(*She hands* LIZZIE *the spoon.*)

MARY: What is your sorrow?

PREGNANT GIRL: A straw in wind.

(*She hands* MARY *the straw.*)

MARY: What will the wind carry?

PREGNANT GIRL: The bone of a child.

(*She hands* MARY *the bone. She raises the cauldron and the bayonet.*)
I'll hold on to these. Value what you're given. They'll be
useful one day.

LIZZIE: What for?

PREGNANT GIRL: That would be telling.

LIZZIE: Tell.

PREGNANT GIRL: Look what happens to those that tell. They get their throats cut.

(*The* PREGNANT GIRL *and the* WOMEN *fade.* MARY *and* LIZZIE *are left alone with their* MOTHER.)

MOTHER: So.

MARY: So.

MOTHER: Well.

LIZZIE: Well.

MOTHER: Your father's in a place called Manchester. Go to him there.

MARY: Why will the famine be let happen?

(*Silence.*)

MOTHER: Anyway, yous better go.

LIZZIE: How will we get there?

MOTHER: Swim.

LIZZIE: I'm afraid of water.

MOTHER: Jesus, two grown women and I still have to do everything for them. Swim.

(*The* MOTHER *licks her hand. She touches the foreheads of* MARY *and* LIZZIE. *Lights fade. Music.*)

LIZZIE: So this is England? Who will we meet here?

MARY: Whoever's in store for us.

LIZZIE: Who do you want to meet?

MARY: Time for a man.

LIZZIE: You, a man? (*Laughs.*) You're half man already, Mary.

MARY: How?

LIZZIE: You could always do a man's work.

MARY: It's only work.

LIZZIE: You'd enjoy a man.

MARY: Would he enjoy me? I think I'd be jealous of him enjoying me. I wouldn't like to be jealous. But I'd like a man. Before I'm ancient. Jesus, age, wouldn't it break your heart?

LIZZIE: Will your heart break?

MARY: Only when I hear it.

LIZZIE: Breaking?

MARY: Beating. What's the difference?

LIZZIE: Poor old Mary, she'll die of love.

MARY: Poor old Mary, she'll die of loneliness.

LIZZIE: What about the man?

MARY: He's still to be found.

   (*A young woman,* QUEEN VICTORIA, *enters. She sees* MARY *and* LIZZIE *and screams.*)

LIZZIE: Jesus, girl, take it easy.

MARY: Take it easy, take it easy.

VICTORIA: Do you mean me any harm?

LIZZIE: No, pet, you're safe enough here.

MARY: Are you being followed?

VICTORIA: Of course, morning, noon and night, they hound me.

LIZZIE: Who?

VICTORIA: My people.

LIZZIE: Your family don't trust you?

VICTORIA: Family? No, my people. They insist I rule. And I'm too young.

MARY: Rule where?

VICTORIA: Are you being amusing? England. I am Queen Victoria, and I wish to die.

LIZZIE: Who's Queen Victoria?

VICTORIA: Me. Don't be overawed. A simple curtsey will suffice.

MARY: How do you want to die?

VICTORIA: Drowning.

MARY: Well, you're dressed for it.

VICTORIA: I always am. State occasions demand it. God, I'm knackered by state occasions. Still, England demands, England demands, England demands . . . too much. A cruel mother, this country. Pushing, watching, pushing, all the time. England.

LIZZIE: What's it like, England?

VICTORIA: Aren't you English?

MARY: We've just come from the water.

VICTORIA: Good gracious, are you mermaids? Where are your tails?

(VICTORIA *sniggers*.)

LIZZIE: Watch your fucking mouth, lady.

VICTORIA: You wouldn't talk to me like that if Lord Melbourne were here.

MARY: He's not.

LIZZIE: What put a man into your head?

VICTORIA: There's nothing between us. I am not an adultress. I swear it before God and man. (*Throws herself on her knees*.) I am a good, clean, respectable girl, saving herself for marriage. There is nothing between me and my Prime Minister. He could be a woman for all I care. Tittle-tattle, tittle-tattle.

MARY: Tittle-tattle.

LIZZIE: Tittle-tattle.

VICTORIA: You don't believe me?

MARY: We do.

LIZZIE: Millions don't.

MARY: But we do.

LIZZIE: You're the talk of the town.

MARY: Down under the ocean.

LIZZIE: Young mermaids aren't allowed to mention your name.

MARY: Blush at the sound of it.

LIZZIE: Tails grow quite red.

MARY: Shocking to fish and fin.

LIZZIE: You count for nothing down there, girl.

VICTORIA: Nothing?

LIZZIE: Nothing.

VICTORIA: You mean if I were to leap into the sea and sink to the bottom of your kingdom – you have a king, I take it?

MARY: No.

VICTORIA: Down to your – your republic – hateful word – I would be –

MARY: Ignored.

VICTORIA: Oh. So it's only on the earth I command respect? Well then, that settles it. I'd better gobble up a lot more of it than this sceptred isle, this seat of Mars, this teeming womb of kings. Methinks I am a prophet, newly blessed. I will see the lands of England swirl before me like a skirt, lifting me and my people through the continents of the earth. Which part of my expanding empire would you mermaids wish to conquer?

LIZZIE: Manchester.

VICTORIA: Why?

LIZZIE: Do you know it?

VICTORIA: I've smelt it.

LIZZIE: What's it like?

VICTORIA: Words rarely fail me. They do not on this occasion. An open sewer, Manchester.

LIZZIE: We're searching for our father.

VICTORIA: I know what you mean.

LIZZIE: Our mother's dead.

VICTORIA: The poor have all the luck.

MARY: What will you do?

VICTORIA: I'm born to rule. My destiny, England's destiny, decreed by God, by fate and by me. A myth I am, but not yet a monster. There will be wonderful stories about my terrible life. As a child, they dressed me in black. It was in preparation. Not for being queen, but for being a woman. What is England like? Go and find out. I can tell you one thing. It isn't content. So it roams the world, looking for contentment. And finds it nowhere. For no one wants it. That's a secret between me and the empire. Put it under your hat, when you can afford one. I worry for poor England when the wandering's over. Where will it go then but into itself, and what will it find? A tenement. The England that was wont to conquer others now makes a conquest of itself. Some third-rate isle lost among her seas. How shall we cope? By lying, I suppose. Methinks I am a prophet newly blessed. The old order changeth, yielding place to the new. Find it. Find it in Manchester. Would you excuse me? I must rule. I have an empire to govern. May as well enjoy it while it lasts. I send best wishes to your kingdom under the sea. We must exchange ambassadors. I'll speak to Lord Melbourne. (*Moves to exit.*) Forgive me.

MARY: Why?

VICTORIA: I don't know. I felt like asking. Forgive me.

(VICTORIA *exists*.)

LIZZIE: Rare bird, her.

MARY: She'll get over it. To Manchester.

ENGELS: You know something, Karl?

(MARX *continues writing*.)

Yours is the first circumcised cock I've ever seen.

MARX: What has brought my – penis – into your conversation?

ENGELS: Well, for two men, and you'd agree on this, Karl, two men so much into materialism, it seems to me like a waste of good skin.

MARX: Frederick, at the time it happened I had not as yet evolved my political theories.

(ENGELS *laughs*.)

Is this some kind of joke?

ENGELS: Yes.

MARX: I am not amused.

(*Silence*.)

ENGELS: What are you doing?

MARX: Writing a poem.

ENGELS: To your wife?

(*Silence*.)

To a friend like me?

MARX: In a way. It is for the benefit of all mankind.

ENGELS: What's it about?

MARX: A profound experience of my own. My conversion to the materialist conception of history.

ENGELS: That should be good. What do you call it?

MARX: It doesn't have a title.

ENGELS: That's bloody daft. Poem needs a title, part of a poem, title. Stupid bloody poem, no title. I don't like it already.

MARX: Why do you want a title?

ENGELS: I like to know where I stand. Could I run a business unless it had a name? Ermen and Engels, Number 2, South Gate, Deansgate, Manchester. Textile Manufacturers. Jesus, Karl, you want to change the world and you can't be trusted to give your poem a title.

MARX: Sometimes I think you are quite mad.
   (*Silence*.)
ENGELS: I'm sorry. I apologize.
MARX: I accept.
   (*Silence*.)
ENGELS: Read the poem.
MARX: To please you, I shall call it 'Ode to Materialism'.
ENGELS: I like that.
MARX: Thank you.
ENGELS: Read it.
MARX: 'Material powers of production, I salute you'.
   (*Silence*.)
ENGELS: Is that it?
MARX: Yes.
ENGELS: It's very good. Very unlike you. Concise. To the point.
   'Material powers of production, I salute you'. Keep going.
   How about, 'The bourgeois relations of production are the
   last antagonist form of the social process of production –
   antagonistic not in the sense of individual antagonism but of
   one arising from conditions surrounding the life of
   individuals in society'?
MARX: That doesn't rhyme.
ENGELS: No, it wouldn't, you see. It's only one line. The next
   line could be something like, 'At the same time the
   productive forces developing in the womb of bourgeois
   society create the material conditions for the solution of that
   antagonism. This social formation constitutes therefore the
   closing chapter of the prehistoric stage of human society.'
MARX: Perhaps we should stick to prose.
ENGELS: No, no, I'm off on this poetry lark. We end every line
   with the word society to underline man as social being. Get
   it?
MARX: Go to sleep, Engels.
ENGELS: Are you afraid of the dark?
MARX: No.
ENGELS: I am.
MARX: Why?
ENGELS: Dreaming.

MARX: Why are you afraid of dreaming?

ENGELS: It might come true, the dream.

MARX: I don't understand you.

ENGELS: You do. You know the way you walk for miles through somewhere you know, but you see nothing, for you're lost inside your own head? I do that. I'm lost. I'm lonely. In a funny way it's why I love the poor. I think they're lonely too. Do you love the poor?

MARX: I hate them. I hate your sentimental waffle about them. I hate their ignorance. I hate their cruelty. I hate their stupidity. I hate their patience. I hate you for loving them. I hate you for drinking with them, laughing with them. I hate the poor.

ENGELS: Lightens the load, a good laugh.

MARX: The load is not to be lightened. Not to be lifted. The load's there to be carried. The poor are beasts of burden. I won't ease the burden, but the beasts can be released on civilization, and when they are freed, they will shake the world to its very foundations. So the poor are lonely? No, no one is lonely, no one. Tired, broken, despairing, destroyed, yes, but not lonely. There's no such thing as loneliness. Or at least there won't be, in our future.

ENGELS: Are you sure?

MARX: Are you not?

ENGELS: Yes. (*Cuddles up to* MARX.) Do you know 'The Sleeping Beauty'?

MARX: Why?

ENGELS: My favourite.

MARX: It's a girl's story.

ENGELS: Suppose it is.

MARX: I'm going to sleep.

ENGELS: You know, I like girl's stories. I like girls. I should find a girl.

MARX: A witch.

ENGELS: What?

MARX: A wicked witch. Like mine.

ENGELS: Jenny?
(*Silence.*)

Are you asleep? I'm afraid of the dark. Demons, dragons, but not witches, funny enough.
(*Silence*.)
Not very rational, is it? If you were awake, you'd laugh me out of it. No, you'd argue me out of it. Just like my father. Arguing. It was my mother who laughed. Father, always arguing. Father. That's why I'm afraid of ghosts. Spectres. Haunting me.
(MARX *rises and sleepwalks*. ENGELS *sings low*.)

It is the dead of night,
The house is full,
My father's in the house,
He eyes my mother.

Rather her than us,
Rather her than us.
Haunts me to my grave,
To my grave, haunted.

Rather her than us,
He eyes my mother,
Father in the house,
Haunts me to the grave.

(*Silence*. MARX *moves to exit*.)
Where are you walking in your sleep, Karl? Back to your wife?
(MARX *exits*.)
I'd like to kill my father. I wouldn't call it murder. I'd call it war. You would approve of that. I like approval. I'll send you money, Karl. It's his for the taking. My father's, that is. I'm afraid of my father, even if he's dead and gone. He haunts me through Germany, through France and England. He haunts the whole of Europe. A ghost, a spectre. There may be no escape. For him, as well as me. Night night, Father. Night night, Karl. Night night, Europe. Night, night night.

ight changes. MARY *and* LIZZIE *enter. Music.* ENGELS *sees them.*

MARY: Are you afraid of the night?
LIZZIE: Are you afraid to dream?
MARY: Do you see in your dreams?
LIZZIE: Will you see with us?
ENGELS: Who are you?
LIZZIE: Will you walk with us?
MARY: Through Manchester?
LIZZIE: Can we ask our father?
MARY: He works in Manchester.
LIZZIE: Will you hold his hand?
MARY: Will you walk with us?
LIZZIE: Through Manchester?
MARY: Will we show you Manchester?
LIZZIE: The poor of Manchester?
MARY: Will we show you our father?
LIZZIE: Will you hear our father?
ENGELS: Who are you?
MARY: Witches.
LIZZIE: Poor women.
MARY: Are you lonely?
LIZZIE: Are you rich?
MARY: Do you live in a palace?
LIZZIE: In a mansion?
MARY: Is it your father's mansion?
LIZZIE: Our father lived there.
MARY: In your palace.
LIZZIE: In your factory.
MARY: Come with us.
LIZZIE: Meet our father.
MARY: Mister Engels of Manchester.
　　(*Industrial sounds pierce. Half-naked, dyed brown,*
　　MICHAEL BURNS, *father to Mary and Lizzie, walks. As the*

29

noise stops, the FATHER *begins to shake. He speaks to his hands, sinking to his knees.*)

FATHER: Will you stop shaking? You're the tools of my trade. Steady yourself, will you? Do you want us to starve? Body, will you have wit? What kind of humour's in you? Will you turn me blue with want? Is there anyone listening? Is there one to hear me? Body, stop shaking? Will you lead me to the workhouse?

(FATHER *sings.*)

FATHER: Fingers to the bone, fingers to the bone,
　　　　Walk through shite on your way back home.
　　　　Skies shite rain, rain shites on all,
　　　　Mouth to feed, hunger on the wall.
　　　　Army on its stomach, poor like night,
　　　　Marching, marching, brown as shite.

　　　　Women in this town, breasts laced with milk,
　　　　Men in this town, dry enough to drink.
　　　　Them in this town churn that milk to butter,
　　　　Sell it back with salt to milking mother.
　　　　Sweat from your brow earns the daily bread,
　　　　Bread black as sweat, dyed body red.

(*Silence.*)

Is there one out there?

(ENGELS *holds out his hand.*)

Is anyone listening?

(ENGELS *begins to raise his hand.* FATHER *begins to rise from the ground.*

Is there one to hear me?

(FATHER *is now on his feet.* ENGELS *looks at his hand.* ENGELS *sings.*)

ENGELS: Kill the scavengers that fly,
　　　　Above the streets of Manchester,
　　　　Owl and kite that guide their cries
　　　　Throughout the streets of Manchester,
　　　　Devouring pain red as meat,
　　　　Raw on the streets of Manchester.

(FATHER *sings.*)

FATHER: Kill the bird, the pain, the sheet
That winds the streets of Manchester.
Into profit, loss and gain,
The shroud of streets of Manchester.
(ENGELS *sings*.)
ENGELS: The factory that bears my name
Opens the streets of Manchester,
Lead me through the lasting shame
That moves through streets of Manchester.
(MARY *sings*.)
MARY: Body, build the factory brown
That made the streets of Manchester.
(LIZZIE *sings*.)
LIZZIE: Body, tear the factory down,
Deface the streets of Manchester.
(*The* FATHER *looks at his hands. They shake violently*.)
FATHER: Press. Press. Watch the wheel, the rope's slackening.
Press, girl, press. Watch the room. For warmth, for wet. If
the thread snaps, the machine stops. Never let the machine
stop. Never let the hand stop. Press, woman, press. Watch
the thread winding. For Christ's sake, watch the thread
winding. Man is his machine, woman's work is never done.
Keep your eyes peeled to the thread. Wind your eyes out
from your body. Man's body's woman's work. Sore eyes,
sore hand, sore work, sore body. I want to work, I want to
die, I need to wash the dirt off myself. I need to die.
(*The* FATHER *fades*.)
ENGELS: Are you afraid of the dark?
MARY: No.
LIZZIE: No.
ENGELS: Will you live with me?
MARY: Together.
LIZZIE: Together.
ENGELS: Are you afraid of changing the whole wide world?
MARY: We've met the man.
LIZZIE: Kind.
MARY: Good.
LIZZIE: Then the match is made, till death do us part.

31

MARY: Sisters in life.

LIZZIE: Sisters in love.

ENGELS: Living with Frederick Engels.

(ENGELS *stands between* MARY *and* LIZZIE. *They link arms.*
They walk back and forth.)

LIZZIE: Years ago in this country they say two women met a man
and they went walking through Manchester. The women
gave the man safe passage through the dangerous poor, for
he believed in changing the workings of the world, and
because they loved this world, they believed in him. They
showed him the poor and they showed him their father and
they showed their race and themselves to him, the two
women, Mary and Lizzie Burns, sisters in life, sisters in love,
living with Frederick Engels, for they believed in the end of
the world. Listen to the world changing. Listen to the world
ending.

(*They look at each other.*)

MARY *and* LIZZIE *have equipped themselves with fans.*

MARX: The value form, whose fully developed shape is the money
     form –
MARY: Money?
MARX: Yes. It is very elementary and simple.
MARY: Simple.
MARX: Yes. Nevertheless the human mind –
LIZZIE: Mind?
MARY: Human?
MARX: Yes. The human mind has for more than 2,000 years
     sought in vain to get to the bottom of it, while on the other
     hand –
LIZZIE: Hand?
MARY: The other.
LIZZIE: Yes.
MARX: To the successful analysis of much more composite and
     complex forms there has been an approximation –
LIZZIE: Why?
MARX: Because the body –
MARY: The body?
LIZZIE: I like the body.
MARY: Yes.
MARX: As an organic whole –
LIZZIE: Legs.
MARX: Is easier to study –
MARY: Tits.
MARX: Than are the cells of that body.
MARY: Body.
LIZZIE: Legs.
MARY: Tits.
LIZZIE: Frederick's more of a tits man than a leg man. Which are
     you, Karl?
     (*Silence.*)

MARX: In the analysis of economic forms, moreover, neither microscopes nor chemical reagents are of use.

ENGELS: I don't mind a bit of leg as well, Lizzie.

MARX: The force of abstraction must replace both.

MARY: Abstraction?

MARX: But in bourgeois society –

(MARY *rapidly interrupts*.)

MARY: The commodity form of the product of labour on the value form of the commodity is the economic cell form. To the superficial observer the analysis of these forms seems to turn upon minutiae. It does in fact deal with minutiae. But they are of the same order as those dealt with in microscopic anatomy, and you can quote me on that one, Karl.

MARX: You are in fact quoting me.

MARY: Aren't you the intimidating, smart boy?

MARX: If I bore you ladies, my wife –

LIZZIE: Are you married?

MARX: You know I am.

MARY: I'd love to be married.

LIZZIE: So would I, but he won't have us. You shame us, Frederick, you're a disgrace.

MARY: No, he's a man of principle. He has no wife.

LIZZIE: Karl has.

MARY: Well, he would.

LIZZIE: I like his wife.

MARY: So does he.

LIZZIE: So does everybody.

MARY: Karl had better be careful. Our bourgeoisie, not content with having the wives and daughters of the proletarians at their disposal, not to speak of common prostitutes –

LIZZIE: Stop, I feel faint.

MARY: – take the greatest pleasure in seducing each other's wives.

LIZZIE: Are you worried about her and Frederick?

MARY: Nah, she has no tits.

LIZZIE: She has legs.

MARY: Have you ever seen them? One night I looked up her skirt. There was a gap between the ground and her knees.

LIZZIE: Poor Jenny.

MARX: These women are not welcome in my house.

ENGELS: I think they know, Karl.

MARX: Then why do you insist on bringing them?

ENGELS: They insist on coming.

LIZZIE: We wouldn't miss it.

MARY: We're respectable women, visiting friends.

LIZZIE: Having dinner.

MARY: Dinner with Karl and Jenny.

LIZZIE: Lovely.

MARY: Not really. We bought it.

(*Silence.*)

MARX: I have frequently acknowledged my friend's financial assistance.

MARY: Then why do you look at his women with poison in your face?

MARX: You are not his women, you are his whores.

LIZZIE: So are you.

MARY: So we're equal. All equal. All respectsble. Tell your wife.

LIZZIE: Where is she?

MARX: Indisposed.

(*Silence.*)

Her nerves.

(*Silence.*)

Every day she wishes she were in the grave. She has grown old. I can no longer cope with her complaining. No, not complaining. Her fantasies.

MARY: Can she cope with yours?

MARX: I have no fantasies.

MARY: No, you have philosophies. Good philosophers, the two of you. Bright as buttons. Brains to burn. Tell me your philosophy, Frederick.

ENGELS: Mary, you're being cruel and stupid.

MARY: Cruel, yes, you sometimes deserve it, but stupid, never, you wouldn't let me, so tell me your philosophy.

ENGELS: For you to mock?

MARY: For me to hear.

ENGELS: And when you hear, have your laugh?

MARY: No laugh. I'll listen. Tell me your philosophy.

35

ENGELS: Division into classes has a certain historical justification. It has this only for a given period under given social conditions. It was based upon the insufficiency of production.

(MARY *begins to open* ENGELS's *fly*.)

It will be swept away by the complete development of modern productive forces.

(LIZZIE *goes behind* ENGELS *and strokes his hair. His fly is now undone*.)

ENGELS: What the hell are you doing?

MARY: Listening.

LIZZIE: Go on.

ENGELS: And in fact the abolition of classes in society presupposes a degree of historical evolution at which the existence –

MARY: Existence.

(MARY's *mouth moves towards* ENGELS's *fly*. LIZZIE *kisses his forehead*.)

ENGELS: Not simply of this or that ruling class, but of any ruling class at all –

LIZZIE: You like being ruled sometimes. You love it.

MARX: My God.

(ENGELS *begins to grow agitated*.)

ENGELS: Class distinction itself has become an anachronism.

LIZZIE: Hold a grip on yourself, man.

ENGELS: Intellectual leadership –

(LIZZIE *slaps* ENGELS's *face*.)

LIZZIE: Don't rush, take it easy.

ENGELS: – by a particular class of society has become not only superfluously but economically –

LIZZIE: Politically – Intellectually –

ENGELS: – a hindrance to development.

(ENGELS *reaches climax. He roars*.)

That point has now been reached.

(LIZZIE *kisses* ENGELS. MARY *holds both in her arms. They kiss* MARY. LIZZIE *climbs on* ENGELS's *shoulders*. MARY *gets herself between his legs*. ENGELS *howls with pleasure*. JENNY *enters, carrying a teatray. On the tray are a dish of strawberries, a vase of flowers and two sheets of paper*.)

JENNY: Tea?

ENGELS: Excuse us, Jenny. I was just illustrating to the company the distinction between utopian and scientific socialism.

LIZZIE: I'm utopian; she's scientific.

(MARY *and* LIZZIE *release themselves from* ENGELS.)

JENNY: Really? Would you care for a strawberry?

MARX: We were expecting dinner, my love.

JENNY: There will be no dinner, my sweet.

MARX: Why not, my angel?

JENNY: You don't believe in angels, my lamb.

MARX: I believe in you, my swan.

JENNY: Thank you, my deer.

MARX: Where is dinner, my spaniel?

JENNY: There is no food, my ox.

MARX: Why not, my owl?

JENNY: We have no money, my camel.

MARX: Frederick provided us with money, my sick lioness.

JENNY: I burned it, my hawk.

MARX: Why?

JENNY: It was given to me by a tainted hand.

MARY: Mine.

JENNY: By a tainted mind.

MARY: Mine.

JENNY: I do not like you in my house.

MARY: I don't like you in your house.

JENNY: You gentlemen see fit to entertain these women. How different we are as a species, male, female and those between both. Excuse me, I will adjourn to my room –

MARY: And go mad.

(*Silence.*)

JENNY: You cunt.

MARY: *You* cunt.

LIZZIE: Three cunts.

(*Silence.*)

ENGELS: Tea?

(MARY *lifts the vase of flowers. She removes the flowers from the vase. She drinks the water from the vase. She throws the flowers at* JENNY's *feet.*)

37

JENNY: Thank you.

(MARY *and* LIZZIE *bow to* JENNY. JENNY *bows back. She walks to* MARX *with the tray. He takes the tray from her.*)

Offer our guests food, husband. I apologize for the poverty of the fare, but the dish is beautiful. I like to look at it. It convinces me I am a wealthy woman.

(*They each take a strawberry and eat.*)

As a young woman, I was quite pretty. Do eat more strawberries, they're quite delicious. Forgive my nerves. I bought the strawberries all by myself. Are you proud of me, Karl? Karl has lived with my nerves so long he scarcely notices them. I drive him out of the house. He is a good man, I've made him what he is today. We love each other. For him I would pawn my life. Which is just as well. It is the only thing we have not pawned yet. (*Laughs.*) My strength is I find it all so funny. Karl Marx cannot feed his family; his wife and mainstay cannot help her husband. Aren't we silly-billies? I do encourage him now with the odd extravagant gesture. That is why I burned the money. Have you ever watched money burning? A piece of paper, turning to ash. I was conducting a scientific experiment. Will it burn to gold? It didn't, Karl. Ash to ash and dust to dust, money is death, my love, and you have been dealing in death for so long, my darling, I have lost direction and you are losing control, for the house is falling about our ears and now I only hear you speak to me in the crumbling walls and squeaking doors and the holes in the roof and your bloody books. I would like to put a match to your books and watch them blaze like an old boot and say, this is my life and if life be a wheel, I am spinning out of control. You cannot help me, husband. Help me. Help me. I am a noble woman. I am wife to Karl Marx, who cannot feed his family but who would feed all mankind. It's a conspiracy against me. You and your whores, Mr Engels, conspire with the world against me. I do realize what is going on around me.

(*Silence.*)

Eat. Eat the strawberries. I picked them myself.

(JENNY *squeezes strawberries in her hands until they are red.*)

When I was young and could look in the mirror, I once saw myself like a tree, and then one night I lit a candle and Karl appeared. I got such a shock. I thought it was my husband, he took my breath away. Perhaps he didn't. We've travelled together through life. To where, I don't know. Do eat these strawberries. To death, I suppose. I picked them myself. (*Looks at her hands.*) I have a mind of my own. Fetch me the tray, Karl.

(MARX *goes to her with the tray.* JENNY *takes the sheets of paper and wipes her hands with them.*)

Read my hands. What's written on the paper. Handwriting. Only I can read your handwriting. Shall I whisper a sinister prophecy of coming catastrophe?

(JENNY *whispers, reading from the crumpled paper.*)

All fixed, fast-frozen relations with their train of ancient and venerable prejudices and opinions are swept away, all new-formed ones become antiquated before they can ossify. All that is solid melts into air, all that is holy is profaned, and man is at last compelled to face with sober senses his real contradictions of life and his relations with his kind. (*Silence.*)

Well, are you proud of your wife? Did you believe she'd think that up? I wrote that, not you, my love. Isn't this my handwriting?

(MARX *turns from her.*)

Solid, melting into air, my husband. Holy, now profaned, our life. His sober senses recoil from me. Face me, face your kind. Am I your contradiction? Are we not speaking? My husband and I are in opposition tonight. I am afraid he will brand me revolutionary. Well, it is high time revolutionaries should openly, in the face of the whole world, publish their views, their aims, their tendencies, and meet this nursery tale –

(MARX *grabs the paper from her.*)

MARX: A nursery tale is right. You reduce me and my work to your handwriting. You are ridiculous, Jenny –

JENNY: No, I am redundant. A useless piece of production, past child-bearing, and there were no sons –

MARX: I love my daughters.

JENNY: There were no sons. When you're silent, I can read your lips. They curse me in Hebrew. I can read your mind. Every word you've written, I've thought before you.

MARX: That is lying. That is fantasy.

(JENNY *takes out notes of money*.)

JENNY: Is this? I didn't burn it. There I was lying. But I will if you don't help me. (*Drops a note.*) Pick it up. (*Drops another note.*) Pick it up. (*Drops another note.*) Pick it up.

(MARX *collects the money*.)

My husband understands money. It grows on the tree. You are so kind, Frederick. I love you for your cruel kindness. I find you so funny. My husband finds you useful. Do you girls find him useful or funny? Do you love him for his money? You know how money talks. Have you heard how he talks about you? Have you seen what he's written?

MARY: We don't read.

JENNY: Shall I tell you what he's said?

LIZZIE: He's never mentioned our name.

JENNY: He's named your race, however. Do you think he loves you? Listen to 'The Condition of the Working Class'. This extract is so amusing. 'Drink is the only thing which makes the Irishman's life worth living. His crudity which places him but little above the savage, his filth and poverty, all favour drunkenness. The temptation is great, he cannot resist it, and so when he has money he gets rid of it down his throat.' (*Laughs loudly.*) Forgive me, it is so amusing. You would agree there is some truth in it. Don't you find it funny? Shall I read on? 'With such a competitor the English working man has to struggle, with a competitor on the lowest plane possible in a civilized country, who for this reason requires less wages than any other. All such as demand little or no skill are open to the Irish. For work which requires long training or regular, pertinacious application, the dissolute, unsteady, drunken Irishman is on too low a plane.'

LIZZIE: Read on.

JENNY: I can't, you don't find it funny.

40

MARY: (*Sings*) My young love said to me, My father won't mind,
And my mother won't slight you for your lack of kine,
And she moved away from me and this she did say,
It won't be long, love, until our wedding day.

LIZZIE: (*Sings*) The people were saying, no two were 'er wed,
But one had a sorrow that never was said,
And she moved away from me with one star awake,
Like a swan in the evening moves over the lake.

MARY: Read on.

ENNY: 'When, in almost every city, a fifth or a quarter of the
workers are Irish, or children of Irish parents, who have
grown up amid Irish filth, no one can wonder if the life,
habits, intelligence, moral status – in short the whole
character of the working class assimilates a great part of the
Irish characteristics.

MARY and LIZZIE: (*Sing*) Last night she came to me, my dead
love crept in,
She crept in so softly, her feet made no din.
As she moved away from me, these words she did say,
It will not be long, love, until our wedding day.

MARY: (*Sings alone*) Last night she came to me, my dead love,
my dead love.
(*Silence.*)

ENGELS: You know it's the truth.
(*Silence.*)
You know what you showed me.

MARY: Mo ghrá thú, lá da bhfacha thú.

LIZZIE: I loved, the day I saw you.

MARX: You're dangerous, a rotting mass, sitting there, passive,
the lowest of the low, you might have your uses, you could
be swept into life, but in your condition you're part and
parcel of the old regime.

LIZZIE: And you offer us a bun, we lick the sugar but throw
away the bread, is that it?

MARY: We'd fail you, yes?

MARX: Yes.

MARY: As you've failed us?

ENGELS: I've never failed.

MARY: You have failed me.

ENGELS: I have never failed.

MARY: What's the fear in you?

ENGELS: Fear?

MARY: Us? Our like? Is that behind it all? You don't know us. You fear us. So you'll remove us. The breastbeaters would save our souls for the sake of their own salvation. How will you save us? Change the world, eh? Change us. Change yourself first. Mr Engels is afraid of the dark. We're the dark. We're the night. Will I show you the dark? Will I lead you through the night to come?

ENGELS: Have you lost your reason?

MARY: It's dead, reason.

JENNY: Dead love.

MARX: It's begun to live.

LIZZIE: Dead as a doornail.

JENNY: Dead.

MARX: On the contrary it shall open doors and it shall knock down palaces, the doors of prisons. In the prisons of the mind we shall construct the palaces of freedom –

JENNY: I should like to see this night to come.

(MARY *gives* JENNY *a stone*.)

MARY: Worn like a stone, here is your charm. Fade.

(JENNY *fades*. MARY *gives* MARX *a straw*.)

Name be broken, sacred, profaned, scatter throughout the wide earth. Fade.

(MARX *fades*. MARY *gives* ENGELS *the book wrapped in rags*.)

Through you be I remembered, live when I die. Fade.

(ENGELS *fades*. LIZZIE *stirs the air with the spoon*.)

LIZZIE: Who are we calling?

MARY: Whoever comes.

LIZZIE: What will we give them?

MARY: What they give us.

LIZZIE: What if it's nothing?

MARY: Then so be it.

LIZZIE: How do we get there?

MARY: Making a wish.

LIZZIE: With what?

MARY: A human bone.
(MARY *raises the bone.*)
Let us enter the night to come.
(*The* PREGNANT GIRL *enters.*)
PREGNANT GIRL: Shall I show you the night? Shall I show you
your heart? I heard your heart breaking.

A boy enters. He speaks in Russian.

BOY: *Вы нас видите?*
PREGNANT GIRL: Can you see us? Yes, I can.
BOY: *Вы можете это описать?*
PREGNANT GIRL: Can you describe this? Yes, I can.
BOY: *Вы помните утро и ночь?*
PREGNANT GIRL: Do you remember morning and night? That's
    when they came, morning and night.
BOY: *Это когда они пришли, утром и ночью, вошли в
    дверь, посмотрели на мою маму.*
PREGNANT GIRL: Came through the door, looked at my mother.
BOY: *Моя мама хочет попить воды.*
PREGNANT GIRL: My mother would like a drink of water.
BOY: *Она головой ударяется об пол, степи России.*
PREGNANT GIRL: Her head hits the floor, the steppes of Russia.
BOY: *Она плачет за всю Россию.*
PREGNANT GIRL: She is crying through the whole of Russia.
BOY: *Они застрелили моего отца, его надо похоронить.*
PREGNANT GIRL: They've shot my father, he has to be buried.
BOY: *У моей мамы кровь течёт, я должен её найти.*
PREGNANT GIRL: My mother's bleeding, I have to find her.
    (*The* BOY *speaks in English.*)
LIZZIE: Where will we find your mother?
BOY: Where there are women walking.
LIZZIE: Where will we find your father?
BOY: Inside my mother.
MARY: What will we tell them?
BOY: Listen.
    (*The* BOY *weeps.*)
MARY: Why do you look at me like that?
LIZZIE: Where are we?
    (*The* BOY *fades.* MARY *stands in silence.*)
    Mary?

(*Silence.*)
What are you hearing?
(*Silence.*)
What are you seeing?
MARY: Women walking.
       (*The* WOMEN OF THE CAMPS *enter. They sing in chorus.*)
CHORUS: Comb not your hair,
          Wash not your face,
          Earth through your hair,
          Earth on your face,
          Take ye and eat,
          Body and blood,
          Love's left the earth,
          Froze human hearts.
       (*The* PREGNANT GIRL *hits the cauldron with the bayonet.*)
FIRST WOMAN: Have you seen my son,
          Wandering the forest?
          I found my son's blood
          On the leaves of the forest.
          How was it his?
          I was told by the forest.
          I told the earth
          Of crimes in the forest.
          They locked me away,
          But I see the forest.
CHORUS: Take ye and eat,
          Body and blood,
          Love's left the earth,
          Froze human hearts.
       (*The* PREGNANT GIRL *hits the cauldron with the bayonet.*
       The SECOND, THIRD *and* FOURTH WOMEN *sing in*
       chorus.)
SECOND, THIRD *and* FOURTH WOMEN:
          I wrote down my name,
          Lest it be forgotten.
          I hid it in the earth,
          Let it be forgotten.
          I burned it in fire,

45

May it be forgotten.
I drowned it in water,
It was not forgotten,
For air told the earth,
Water's not forgotten.
They locked me from air,
But fire's not forgotten.

(*All the* WOMEN *sing in chorus.*)

CHORUS: Take ye and eat,
Body and blood,
Love's heard the earth,
Healed human hearts.

(*The* PREGNANT GIRL *beats the cauldron with the bayonet. The* FIFTH *and* SIXTH WOMEN *sing.*)

FIFTH *and* SIXTH WOMEN:
I dreamt of my death,
My crime was to dream.
I dreamt of my birth,
I entered my dream.
I woke from my death,
It was their dream.
They crushed my head,
My brain went to dream.
They locked me in sleep,
But I'm still my dream.

CHORUS: Take ye and eat,
Body and blood,
Love's heard the earth,
Healed human hearts.
Take ye and eat,
Body and blood,
Love heard the earth,
Healed human hearts.

(*The* WOMEN *exit.*)

(*The* PREGNANT GIRL *beats wildly on the cauldron with the bayonet. She stops suddenly.*)

PREGNANT GIRL: Too long I've carried this burden inside me. Time to be free.

(*The* PREGNANT GIRL *gently cuts her belly open with the bayonet. She begins to laugh low. From inside her she takes a wooden box. She opens the lid. It is empty. She lets the box fall into the cauldron. She laughs.*)

At long last, I've buried my death.

(*The* PREGNANT GIRL *holds out her hands to* MARY *and* LIZZIE.)

PREGNANT GIRL: Give me back what I gave you.

LIZZIE: We gave it away.

PREGNANT GIRL: Everything?

(LIZZIE *hands her the spoon.*)

You?

(MARY *looks at the bone. She puts it in her mouth. It chokes her. She spits it into her hand.*)

Give it to me, that's not your job.

MARY: What is my job?

(*Silence.*)

Will I never give birth?

(*Silence.*)

Will I always be haunted? Will I always be lonely?

(*Silence.*)

Tell me.

(*The* PREGNANT GIRL *takes the bone and places it in the spoon. She puts bone and spoon in her belly.*)

PREGNANT GIRL: Start again, I suppose. Rough life, eh? No rest, no rest, until the grave. But there's no grave either. Just the earth. Wander it. It is too lonely.

(*The* PREGNANT GIRL *leaves* MARY *and* LIZZIE. *Silence.*)

MARY: Is anyone listening?

(*Silence.*)

Is there one to hear me?

(*Silence.*)

Frederick, when I call, will you not come to me?

(*Silence.*)

Are you not there? I have something to tell you. I remember you. And you will be remembered, because you loved the earth and loved me, little knowing either. I will be remembered by a line in your life. Frederick Engels

47

lived with two Irishwomen, Mary and Lizzie Burns. Little does that tell. Little do they know. Little did we know. You'll fail, but you'll be forgiven, for you loved, and love forgives. Forgive? Love forgets. Forget Frederick. Forget Karl. Forget Jenny. Forget Lizzie. Forget Mary. Their hearts were human, beating, and I hear mine, breaking. The heart, Jesus, the human heart, beating, breaking.

LIZZIE: Mary.

MARY: Leave me.

(*Silence.*)

Leave me.

(*Silence.*)

Leave me.

(LIZZIE *leaves* MARY. MARY *looks about her. She closes her eyes. She bows her head. Strange light fills the stage. The* MOTHER *appears. She opens* MARY's *eyes.*)

MOTHER: Why are you here?

MARY: I died, Ma.

MOTHER: What from?

MARY: Heart.

MOTHER: Pity about you.

MARY: Pity.

MOTHER: I suppose you're looking for something. You wouldn't be here if you weren't.

MARY: What am I going to do?

MOTHER: You can't come in here. I've just cleaned it. You're going back to life. I'll come with you for the laugh. Don't argue with me. I miss the earth. Where's Lizzie?

MARY: She's still alive.

MOTHER: That's handy. Now how do we get back?

MARY: I don't know.

MOTHER: Shut your mouth. I'm thinking. Sing to me.

MARY: Why?

MOTHER: That's how the earth became. That's what I learned here. God didn't make the earth. We sung it. He heard us and joined in. We did it together, creation. There's no difference between God and man, or woman for that matter. Isn't that interesting? Will we head home? Do you

48

want to see me create the earth?

(*The* MOTHER *sings. As she sings,* MARY *walks arm-in-arm with her.*)

 When Lagan streams sing lullabies,
 There grows a lily fair.

(MARY *sings.*)

MARY: The twilight gleam is in her eyes,
 The moon is in her hair.

(MARY *and her* MOTHER *sing together.*)

MARY *and* MOTHER:
 Then like a lovesick leanashaí,
 She has my heart on fire.
 No rest have I nor liberty,
 For love is lord of all.

(LIZZIE *appears. She joins in the song. The three walk, linked, about the stage.*)

MARY, LIZZIE *and* MOTHER:
 No rest have I, nor liberty,
 For love is lord of all.

MOTHER: Well, so be it.
LIZZIE: Aye, so be it.
MARY: So be it.